How to make an Opera Extension

(And Sell it)

Introduction

Welcome to *How to make an Opera Extension (And Sell it)*. If you're interested in creating and selling an Opera extension, you've come to the right place.

What is Opera?

Opera is a web browser developed by Opera Software. It was first released in 1995 and is known for its speed and efficiency. Opera has a dedicated user base and continues to gain popularity as a browser of choice for many users.

What is an Opera Extension?

An Opera extension is a piece of software that adds extra functionality to the Opera browser. Opera extensions can be developed using HTML, CSS, and JavaScript. Extensions can do many things, such as adding new buttons to the Opera toolbar, modifying web pages, or adding features to the browser.

Why create an Opera Extension?

There are many reasons to create an Opera extension. Some developers create extensions to solve a specific problem they have encountered while using the browser. Others create extensions to provide additional functionality that is missing from the browser. And, of course, some developers create extensions as a way to make money. In this book, we'll cover everything you need to know to create and sell your own Opera extension. So let's get started!

WHAT IS OPERA?

Opera is a web browser that was created in 1995 by Jon Stephenson von Tetzchner and Geir Ivarsⵔy at Telenor, a Norwegian telecommunications company. It was initially released for Microsoft Windows, but later versions were also made available for other operating systems such as macOS, Linux, and Android. Opera has many features that set it apart from other browsers, such as integrated messaging services, a built-in VPN, ad-blocking, and a battery saver mode. It also has a sleek design and a customizable interface that allows users to modify the look and feel of the browser to their liking. Opera has a small but dedicated user base, and is especially popular among users who appreciate its focus on privacy and security. If you're interested in developing an Opera extension, it's important to understand the unique features of the browser and how they can be leveraged to improve the user experience.

SETTING UP YOUR DEVELOPMENT ENVIRONMENT

Before you start creating your Opera Extension, you need to make sure you have the necessary software installed on your computer. This includes a code editor and a web browser with the Opera developer tools extension installed. First, choose a code editor that you are comfortable with. Popular options include Visual Studio Code, Atom, and Sublime Text. Once you have selected and installed a code editor, you can proceed to install the Opera developer tools extension. To install the Opera developer tools extension, simply visit the Opera Extension store and search for "Opera developer tools". Once you have found it, click "Add to Opera" to install it. This extension provides powerful tools for debugging and testing your extensions. Additionally, you may want to install a linter or formatter to improve the quality and consistency of your code. This will make it easier to maintain and update your extension in the future. There are many options available for various programming languages, so choose one that is appropriate for your needs. With your development environment set up, you are now ready to start building your Opera Extension. In the next subchapter, we will take a closer look at the anatomy of an Opera Extension.

ANATOMY OF AN OPERA EXTENSION

Understanding the structure of an Opera extension is key to creating a functional and useful product. An Opera extension consists of several components, each of which serves a specific purpose. Firstly, the manifest.json file is the backbone of the extension. It provides critical information such as the name, version, and description of the extension, as well as permissions and other configuration settings. Next, the background script is the backbone of the extension's functionality. This is where most of the code executes behind the scenes, handling user events and API calls. Content scripts are responsible for manipulating the DOM of web pages and injecting custom HTML, CSS, and JavaScript into the page. Options pages allow users to customize the settings of the extension and access additional features. Lastly, images, scripts, and other media used by the extension are located in separate folders, organized and named according to their specific role in the extension. Understanding the structure of an Opera extension is just the first step towards creating a successful and useful extension. The way these components interact with one another is crucial to the overall functionality and user experience of the extension. In the next subchapter, we'll discuss how to create your first Opera extension using this knowledge.

CREATING YOUR FIRST OPERA EXTENSION

Congratulations on making it this far! You're now ready to start creating your first Opera Extension. This is an exhilarating moment, as it marks the beginning of your journey as an Opera Extension developer. To start, you need to create a new folder and give it a name. This will be the root folder of your extension. Next, you must create a few files to get things started. The first file you need to create is manifest.json. This is the file that contains all the metadata for your extension, including its name, version number, description, and more. Here's a basic example of what your manifest.json file might look like: { "manifest_version": 2, "name": "My Opera Extension", "version": "1.0", "description": "A simple Opera Extension that does X", "icons": { "48": "icon.png" }, "permissions": ["tabs", "activeTab"], "background": { "scripts": ["background.js"], "persistent": true }, "browser_action": { "default_icon": "icon.png", "default_popup": "popup.html" } } As you can see, this file is written in JSON format and includes several key components. The manifest_version field specifies the version of the manifest file, while name and description provide information about the extension itself. icons, permissions, background, and browser_action are all important fields that determine how your extension works and what it's capable of. Once you've created your manifest.json file, you'll need to create some additional files to bring your extension to life. These will include JavaScript files that define the behavior of your extension, as well as HTML and CSS files that control its appearance. Don't worry if all of this seems overwhelming at first. Creating your first Opera Extension is a process that takes time and effort, but it's also incredibly rewarding. Stick with it, and before you know it, you'll have a fully functional extension that you can use and share with others.

USING THE OPERA EXTENSION API

The Opera Extension API is a powerful set of tools and interfaces that allow you to interact with Opera and its web pages in unique and exciting ways. In this subchapter, we will cover the basics of using the API and some of the more advanced features you can leverage to create truly exceptional Opera extensions. The first step in using the Opera Extension

API is to obtain an API key. This key is required to access the various functions and interfaces provided by the API, and it is unique to each extension. Once you have your key, you can start exploring the API and its many capabilities. One of the most useful features of the Opera Extension API is the ability to communicate with content scripts. Content scripts are scripts that can run in the context of web pages, allowing you to manipulate the contents of those pages, respond to user actions, and perform other tasks. By sending messages back and forth between your extension and your content scripts, you can create dynamic and responsive interfaces that give your users a seamless browsing experience. Some of the other things you can do with the Opera Extension API include: - Creating custom toolbar buttons and menu items - Accessing and modifying browser settings - Handling browser events such as page loads and tab switches - Storing and retrieving data using browser storage APIs - Communicating with other extensions and native applications To get the most out of the Opera Extension API, it is important to read the documentation carefully and experiment with different interfaces and functions. With a little creativity and the right tools, you can create Opera extensions that are both powerful and intuitive, providing your users with a browsing experience that is both enjoyable and efficient. Overall, the Opera Extension API is a fundamental tool for creating high-quality Opera extensions. By leveraging its many capabilities, you can create unique and powerful extensions that stand out in the crowded world of browser extensions. The next subchapter will dive deeper into creating custom UI and events, so stay tuned!

CREATING CUSTOM UI AND EVENTS

One of the benefits of creating an Opera Extension is the ability to customize the user interface (UI) and events to suit your specific needs. With custom UI, you can create a more personalized experience for your users while making your extension stand out in the Opera Extension Store. To create custom UI for your extension, you'll need to have a good understanding of HTML, CSS, and JavaScript. You should also be familiar with the Opera Extension API and how it can be used to manipulate the UI of your extension. When designing your UI, it's important to keep in mind the usability and accessibility of your extension. You want to create an interface that is easy to use and understand, while also being visually appealing. In addition to custom UI, you can also create custom events that can be triggered by your extension. These events can be used to notify the user of important changes or to perform specific actions within your extension. Overall, creating custom UI and events can help differentiate your Opera Extension from the competition and provide a more personalized experience for your users. Just be sure to keep usability and accessibility in mind when designing your UI and events.

UNDERSTANDING YOUR AUDIENCE

Before you can market your Opera extension, you need to understand your audience. Who are they? What are their needs and pain points? What motivates them to download and use an extension? Answering these questions will help you create an extension that meets the needs and desires of your target audience. To get started, conduct market research to identify your audience's characteristics and behaviors. This may involve surveys, interviews, and focus groups. You can also look at data from competitor extensions and user reviews to learn more about what your audience is looking for. Once you have a better understanding of your audience, you can tailor your extension to meet their needs. This may involve adding features that your audience wants, making your extension more user-friendly, or targeting your messaging to specific demographics. Remember to constantly gather feedback from your users to ensure that your extension continues to meet their needs over time. This will help you build a loyal customer base and increase the chances of your extension being shared via word-of-mouth marketing.

PRICING AND REVENUE MODELS

When it comes to selling your Opera extension, pricing is a crucial consideration. The price you set will determine whether users are willing to pay for your extension, and how much revenue you can generate. In this subchapter, we'll take a closer look at some of the most popular pricing and revenue models for Opera extensions. One common approach is to offer your extension for a one-time fee. This model is straightforward and easy to understand for users. You can set your fee based on the perceived value of your extension or the amount of time and effort you put into developing it. Keep in mind that if you set your price too high, users may be deterred from purchasing your extension. Another option is to offer your extension for free, but request donations from users who appreciate your work. This approach is popular among developers who want to reach a wide audience but don't want to exclude users who can't afford to pay for their extension. By relying on donations, you can generate revenue while maintaining an accessible product. Subscription-based pricing is another approach for Opera extensions. This model involves users paying a recurring fee to access your extension. This approach can provide a steady stream of revenue and incentivize users to continue using your extension over time. However, users may be hesitant to commit to recurring payments, and may seek out alternative extensions that offer one-time payments. Finally, you may consider using a freemium model, where you offer a basic version of your extension for free, and charge for premium features. This model allows you to reach a wide audience while providing additional revenue streams for those who want a more robust experience. However, it can be challenging to convince users to upgrade to the premium version, and the added complexity of managing two separate versions of your extension may be a deterrent. Ultimately, the pricing and revenue model you choose will depend on your goals, your audience, and your personal preferences. Take the time to consider your options and experiment with different approaches to find what works best for you and your Opera extension.

PROMOTING AND SELLING YOUR EXTENSION

After completing the development of your Opera extension, it's now time to promote and sell it to the target audience. This is the most critical stage of creating your Opera extension. If it's promoted and marketed effectively, your extension will reach your target audience and generate a significant amount of revenue. Below are some of the factors that you should consider when promoting and selling your Opera extension.

1. Choose the Right Platform for Distribution

There are different platforms available for promoting and distributing your Opera extension. Some of the popular platforms that you should consider include the Opera Add-ons catalog, Chrome Web Store, and Firefox Add-On Store. Each of these platforms has its own audience, and it's crucial to determine which one is the most popular amongst your target users. By choosing the right platform for distribution, you will be able to reach a broader audience and generate more significant revenue from your extension.

2. Optimize Your Extension Listing Page

The listing page is the face of your extension, and it should effectively communicate your extension's features and functionalities to the potential users. Make sure that your listing page includes a clear and concise description of your extension, its features, and screenshots that showcase your extension in use. You should also ensure that your extension listing is optimized for the target keywords that your users may search for.

3. Leverage Social Media Platforms

Social media platforms such as Twitter, Facebook, and LinkedIn can help you promote your Opera extension to a broader audience. Make sure that you have an active presence on these platforms and try to engage with your potential users actively. You could also create video tutorials or demo videos to show how your extension works, and post them on social media platforms to attract more users.

4. Offer Discounts and Promotions

Offering discounts and promotions is an effective way of attracting more users to download and use your Opera extension. You could offer discounts to the early adopters of your extension or run a special promotion during the holiday season. By offering promotions, you will not only attract more users, but you will also retain your existing users.

5. Monitor User Feedback and Reviews

Monitoring user feedback and reviews is essential for the success of your Opera extension. You should encourage your users to leave feedback and reviews on your extension's listing page. This feedback will help you identify any issues or bugs in your extension and fix them promptly. Positive reviews and feedback will also boost your extension's credibility and attract more users to download and use it.

6. Attend Conferences and Meetups

Attending conferences and meetups related to your extension's niche is an effective way of promoting your Opera extension. You can network with other developers and users in your niche and showcase your extension to them. This will help you gain exposure to your extension and generate more revenue. In conclusion, promoting and selling your Opera extension requires a multifaceted approach. By using the strategies outlined above, you will be able to reach a broader audience and generate significant revenue from your extension.

Chapter 5: Case Studies and Examples

In this chapter, we will take a deep dive into successful Opera extension stories, breakdowns of popular Opera extensions, and lessons from the pros. Studying other successful extensions can be an excellent strategy to learn from their successes and apply similar principles to your extension.

SUBCHAPTER 5.1: SUCCESSFUL OPERA EXTENSION STORIES

There have been many successful Opera extensions that have helped to increase user productivity and enhance the browsing experience. One success story is the "AdBlocker Ultimate" extension. This extension blocks all types of ads, ranging from pop-ups to banners, whilst also being completely free. AdBlocker Ultimate has racked up over 10 million downloads and consistently receives positive user reviews.

Another example is the "Honey" extension. Honey is a free extension that automatically searches for and applies coupon codes when users shop online. This extension has saved users millions of dollars and has been incredibly successful since its launch.

SUBCHAPTER 5.2: BREAKDOWNS OF POPULAR OPERA EXTENSIONS

In this subchapter, we will breakdown some of the most popular Opera extensions currently available. These will include, but not limited to:

Grammarly

Grammarly is a free writing assistant extension that checks for grammar, spelling, and punctuation mistakes. It offers a premium version that comes with additional features such as vocabulary enhancement suggestions, genre-specific writing style checks, and a plagiarism checker. As of

2021, Grammarly has over 10 million active users and consistently ranks as the most popular writing assistant extension.

LastPass

LastPass is a password manager that stores user passwords, usernames, and other log-in credentials. It offers a free and premium version, the latter of which includes additional features such as unlimited sharing and emergency access. LastPass currently has over 20 million users.

SUBCHAPTER 5.3: LESSONS FROM THE PROS

Treat this subchapter as a collection of tips, tricks, and best practices from successful Opera extension developers. These can include things like:

Focus on User Experience

Your extension should be intuitive and easy to use, with as few clicks or actions needed as possible. Consider testing it on multiple devices and ensuring it works seamlessly with Opera.

Develop an Awesome Icon

Your extension's icon is one of the first things users will see, so it's essential to make it eye-catching and memorable. Consider creating multiple icon variations and A/B testing to determine the most effective one.

Keep it Simple

Avoid adding unnecessary and complicated features that can clutter your extension's UI. Instead, focus on delivering one unique and valuable feature that is easy to use. By learning from successful Opera extensions and the tips and tricks from experienced developers, you can develop an extension that provides real value to users and achieves success.

SUCCESSFUL OPERA EXTENSION STORIES

Learning from others is a great way to grow and succeed. In this subchapter, we will look at some successful Opera extensions and the stories behind them. One such extension is "Grammarly" which helps users improve their writing by catching grammar and spelling errors. It was developed by a team of linguists and NLP experts who wanted to make writing easier for everyone. Grammarly quickly gained popularity and was acquired by Blackboard, a leading education technology company, in 2018. Another successful Opera extension is "AdBlock Plus." This extension became popular due to its ability to block annoying ads on websites. It was developed by a company called Eyeo GmbH in 2006 and quickly became a favorite among users. Today, it is available not only for Opera but also for Chrome, Firefox, and Safari browsers. The story of these extensions, among others, show how a simple idea or solution can quickly gain momentum and become widely used. If you're thinking of developing an extension, it's worth looking at successful stories for inspiration and guidance.

BREAKDOWNS OF POPULAR OPERA EXTENSIONS

It's always important to study and analyze successful products in order to learn from them and apply the lessons to your own work. In this chapter, we will take a closer look at some popular Opera extensions and break down their key features and design elements. The first extension we'll explore is AdBlock Plus. This extension has over 50 million users and has become an essential tool for many people who are tired of intrusive online ads. AdBlock Plus allows users to block ads on websites and improves page load speeds. The extension also lets users whitelist certain sites if they want to support them financially through ads. One of the key reasons for AdBlock Plus's success is its easy-to-use interface and effective ad-blocking algorithms. Another popular Opera extension is Pocket. This is a read-it-later app that lets users save articles and other content to read later on any device. Pocket has a simple and clean interface that allows users to organize saved items with tags and includes a powerful search feature. Pocket has over 10 million users and has been recognized for its user-friendly design and functionality. LastPass is another highly popular Opera extension that has over 13 million users. This password manager extension securely stores login credentials and automatically fills them in on sites. LastPass allows users to generate strong passwords and has a browser extension for almost every browser. One of its standout features is its ability to securely share password information with trusted family members or co-workers. In summary, popular Opera extensions such as AdBlock Plus, Pocket, and LastPass have several key features that contribute to their success, including easy-to-use interfaces, effective algorithms, clean design, and useful functionality. Studying these extensions can provide valuable insights for creating your own successful Opera extension.

SUBCHAPTER 5.3: LESSONS FROM THE PROS

Learning from the experience and success of other developers is a great way to improve your skills and knowledge. In this subchapter, we will focus on the lessons from experienced Opera Extension developers who have successfully created and sold their extensions. Lesson 1: Know Your Target Users - Understanding the needs and preferences of your target users is the first step towards creating a successful Opera Extension. You must research and analyze the behavior and interests of your potential audience to create an extension that caters to their needs. Lesson 2: Keep the Design Simple and Intuitive - Users choose Opera Extensions because they offer additional functionality or solve a specific problem. To make your extension user-friendly, keep the design simple and intuitive. The interface must be easy to understand, navigate, and interact with, without requiring a steep learning curve. Lesson 3: Use the Opera Extension API Effectively - The Opera Extension API provides developers with a wide range of tools and resources to create powerful extensions with unique functionality. To create an effective extension, you must understand the API and use it effectively to create a reliable, stable and secure extension. Lesson 4: Regularly Update your Extension - Users expect extensions to be up to date and compatible with the latest version of Opera browser. To maintain the loyalty of your users and stay ahead of the competition, make sure to regularly update and improve your extension, fix any bugs or compatibility issues, and make it more effective and efficient. Lesson 5: Offer Excellent Customer Support - Offering excellent customer support is crucial to maintaining the satisfaction and loyalty of your users. Get feedback from your users, respond to queries promptly, and address their concerns and issues. A satisfied user will not only continue using your extension but also recommend it to others. By following these lessons from experienced Opera Extension developers, you can create and sell a great extension that users love and enjoy using.

Chapter 6: Conclusion and Next Steps

Congratulations! You have successfully completed the journey of creating an Opera Extension and learning how to market and sell it. In this final chapter, we will wrap up this book, summarizing what you have learned, and sharing some ideas on how you can leverage your newfound skills.

SUBCHAPTER 6.1: WHAT YOU LEARNED AND ACHIEVED

Throughout this book, we have covered a lot of ground. You started by learning about Opera and what an Opera extension is. Then, you learned how to set up your development environment, create your first extension, and work with the Opera Extension API. In the advanced topics section, you learned how to create custom UI and events and how to work with data and storage. Finally, in the marketing and monetization chapter, you learned how to understand your audience, price your extension, and promote and sell it. By following these chapters, you have gained a comprehensive understanding of what it takes to create and sell an Opera Extension. You have developed new skills that can help you create extensions for any browser with an extension API. You have also learned some tips and tricks to market and sell your extension successfully to a broader audience.

SUBCHAPTER 6.2: WHERE TO GO FROM HERE

Now that you have learned how to create an Opera Extension, you may be wondering what's next? The answer is simple: keep learning and keep creating. Creating extensions is a fantastic way to put your development skills to use and make some money while doing so. One good starting point is to create extensions for other browsers such as Google Chrome, Firefox or Safari. Each browser has different extension APIs, so you will need to learn new things to create extensions for different browsers. However, the principles of extension development remain the same, and you can apply the same skills you learned in this book. You can also start looking into other ways to monetize your extensions. Some developers create open-source extensions to gain visibility and recognition in the developer community. Others create paid extensions and offer advanced features to users. There are also affiliate programs and advertising opportunities that you can explore. The possibilities are endless, and the best thing about extension development is that it's a never-ending learning journey.

SUBCHAPTER 6.3: FINAL THOUGHTS

Creating and selling an Opera Extension is a challenging task, but it's not impossible. With the right skills, tools, and marketing strategies, you can turn your extension into a successful business. Keep in mind that the key to success is to provide value to your users. We hope that this book has been helpful to you and that you have learned what it takes to create and sell an extension successfully. Remember, everything you have learned in this book can be applied to other browsers with extension APIs. So, what are you waiting for? Get out there and start creating!

SUBCHAPTER 6.1: WHAT YOU LEARNED AND ACHIEVED

Congratulations on making it this far! By reading this book, you have learned the ins and outs of creating an Opera Extension and selling it. You have gained knowledge about setting up your development environment, creating an extension, using the Opera Extension API, customizing UI and events, working with data and storage, understanding your audience, pricing and revenue models, promoting and selling your extension, and much more. You have also learned about successful Opera Extension stories and breakdowns of popular extensions. Hopefully, by now, you have a better understanding of how to create and market a successful extension. Throughout this journey, you have achieved a lot. You have learned new skills, expanded your knowledge, and gained a better understanding of the development process. You have also learned how to market and sell your product, which is essential for any successful business. But most importantly, you have learned how to turn your ideas into reality. The creation of an extension can be a challenging process, but by following the steps outlined in this book, you can achieve your goals and create something that will help others. So, what have you learned? You have learned how to create an Opera Extension and sell it successfully. You have learned about the development process, marketing, and selling your product. You have also learned about successful Opera Extension stories and what makes an extension popular. With this new knowledge, the possibilities are endless. You can now take on new challenges, and create innovative extensions that people will love. Remember, innovation and creativity are the keys to success in the world of Opera Extensions. In the next subchapter, we will discuss where to go from here, and what steps you can take to continue your journey towards creating successful Opera Extensions.

WHERE TO GO FROM HERE

Congratulations on completing this book! By now, you should be armed with a wealth of knowledge on how to create and sell your very own Opera extension. However, there is always more to learn, and more ways to improve your skills as a developer and entrepreneur. If you're looking to take things to the next level, here are some resources and steps you can take:

1. Join the Opera Developer Community

The Opera Developer Community is a great place to connect with other extension developers, get answers to your questions, and stay up-to-date with the latest news and updates from Opera. You can join the community by visiting the Opera Developer portal and signing up.

2. Explore the Opera Extensions Catalogue

Take some time to browse the Opera Extensions Catalogue and see what other developers have created. This can give you ideas for your own extensions, as well as help you understand what types of extensions are popular and in demand.

3. Experiment with new Tools and Technologies

As with any field, the world of extension development is constantly evolving. Take some time to experiment with new tools and technologies, and try to stay up-to-date with the latest trends and best practices. This can help you create better and more innovative extensions, as well as pave the way for future success.

4. Keep Learning and Practicing

Finally, the most important thing you can do is to keep learning and practicing. Whether that means taking online courses, attending workshops and conferences, or simply honing your skills through trial and error, the more you know and the more you practice, the better you will become. Remember, creating and selling a successful Opera extension takes time, dedication, and hard work. But with the right knowledge, tools, and mindset, you too can achieve success in this exciting and rewarding field. Good luck!

Creating an Opera extension is a great way to solve user problems and make money.

To build a successful extension, you should start by identifying a problem that your target audience faces and create an extension that solves it. Once you have a viable extension, focus on user acquisition by optimizing your extension's design, marketing your extension, and using effective pricing strategies. Always keep your customer's needs first and focus on providing value.

ISBN 9798392761708

MASTER
EXCEL

Your Ultimate Guide to Mastering Functions, Formulas, and More!

VIRAJ KAKADIA